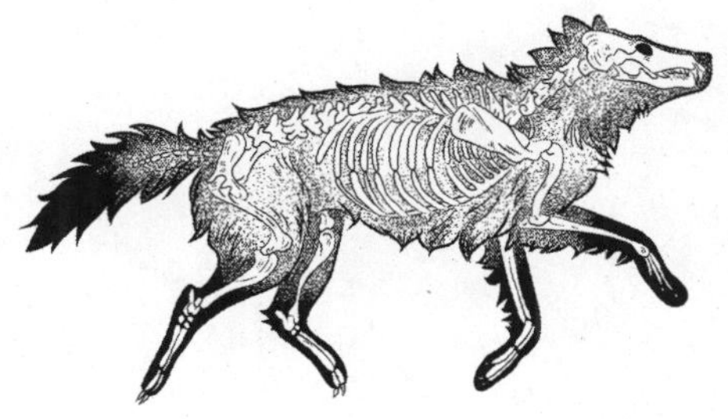

I0821957

AN UNORTHODOX

GUIDE TO WILDLIFE

KATIE VAUTOUR

BREAKWATER
P.O. Box 2188, St. John's, NL, Canada, A1C 6E6
WWW.BREAKWATERBOOKS.COM

A CIP CATALOGUE RECORD FOR THIS BOOK IS AVAILABLE FROM LIBRARY AND ARCHIVES CANADA

ISBN 978-1-55081-768-3
FRONT COVER Skeleton Animal ©Shutterstock

We acknowledge the support of the Canada Council for the Arts, which last year invested $153 million to bring the arts to Canadians throughout the country. We acknowledge the financial support of the Government of Canada and the Government of Newfoundland and Labrador through the Department of Business, Tourism, Culture and Rural Development for our publishing activities.

PRINTED AND BOUND IN CANADA.

Canada Council for the Arts　Conseil des Arts du Canada

Breakwater Books is committed to choosing papers and materials for our books that help to protect our environment. To this end, this book is printed on a recycled paper that is certified by the Forest Stewardship Council®.

TO JOHN BROWNE

AND HIS DAUGHTER,

SUSAN BROWNE,

FOR THEIR INSPIRATION

AND KINDNESS

CONTENTS

BIRD AIRCRAFT STRIKE HAZARD (B.A.S.H.)

Finding himself able,
the cranking Icarus
honks south.

Made of lift and movement,
he disregards conditions,

intersecting the path
of flight AC 667
to Toronto.

He meets the turbine
head-on in
the   tug
                              of air
that won't let go,

pounds and pounds
          of pressure

collapsing breath

as he whips up
into the engine.

Hot steel snaps
                              tendons,
scorches feathers,

melts hollow shafts.

Somewhere under all this,
wrenching bones.

Metal and wire wings depart
skyward as

the bird is cast
back to land.

Moulting liquid light, sun-
                                        burnt fragments
                                                            of desire—
                                        the deep

                    plunge

bringing him

down.

THE OSTRICH

bats
a long-lashed eye.

Hoping for some lift,
puffing
plumage,
she takes off
sprinting.

Her reverse-pedalling
legs go about this
the wrong way—
tripping,
she stops
in her flight.

The ostrich bends
over
backwards,
fixing fly-aways,
ruffling her feather-
duster skirt,
her maid's outfit. Her make-up,

really, is avian, but inside

her head is nothing but bald
lies.

She's an old broad
bird
who should brush off
lofty dreams,

but she's always lived
with her head in the clouds
nestled
around
her neck.

THE BUFFALO IS A PUZZLING CREATURE

For he chews cud like farmers chew tobacco.
For he is lazy, shaking his head free of flies,
saliva stringing in dirt—
            then angry, head tilting,
eyes rolling, nostrils siphoning air.
For he teeters as if he might topple,
then swivels
            like a skittering office chair.
For his great weight sways on spindle legs
gathering in
flows   and charges   and gallops,
ground resounding under hooves.
For when you perch on his hump,
he is not shambling Quasimodo
but a brown moss-coated mountain.
For his horns and head are both battering ram
and brush, flicking snow-dust off shrubs.
For there is a town named after him, but he's never
                                                been there.
For he cannot wield a sabre,
            nor does he resemble a tiger.
For when he quivers he is the rare buffalo, chicken.
For humans roll down car windows quick as he rolls
                                                across plains.

For he inspires red paintings on the rocks of caves.
For his name is not Bill.
For he cannot dance, though many dance in his honour.
For he shrugs off his winter coat for a light summer
sweater.
For his dark eyes are sharp but he needs glasses.
For being almost extinct, then nowhere near extinct.
For feigning true buffalo genes like his African cousins.
For disguising the fact he is a bison.

GARGOYLE

The sky floats heavy above

the vulture

                circling sand,
        narrowing
        his orbit
to a flimsy tin roof.

        Perching
in the middle, pinning
        earth to sky,
        he listens.

Pulsating
        yellow grass
scissors wind.   Weeds whisper

prayers at skeletal
palms.

Drips
trickle
over sticks,
shiny bits
of scrap metal
stacked into a ram-
shackle house.

Rivulets spit
over paint-spattered
steel like
erratic hits of
typewriter
keys.
Raindrops

drum
the hut
buckling

under thunder
clouds.

Lightning arcs: welding
through foundry smoke.

Steam-
breathing buttress
tucks up, torpid:

hook nose below
shoulders.

Satiated,
the winged gargoyle
digests, the putrid
gut bulging—he guards
the tumble-
down. Pour-
ing
rain
funnels,

flourishing,
into gutters.

STREET FOOD

After surviving shots
of clear mescal,
tourists bite frantically
into charred sticks
sold by vendors
on the crooked street.

A gaunt dog staggers
from shadows, snaps
roast meat,
then lurches under

windowpanes staring filthily
down at doorways with
grotesque knockers

where a withered woman
scrapes prickly pear:
spades of stegosaurus tails.

Palms shaking
flies from green flesh
oozing juice
into bowls of grasshoppers
smashed squat with a pestle,
she mixes moles, chilies and salsa.

Over clay cooktops, quivering
funhouse figures
conjure magic,

drizzling liquid
over oil barrels.

Sizzling,
a single curl of smoke

whooshes

into a flashing phoenix.

Soft criss-crossing flames
cast shadows
at all angles and levels

on walls—geckos rise,
fugitives from the fire.

BIRDWATCHER

He rakes embers
from the night before

then cranes his neck

to catch signs
of shadows

rushing above his head:

the gradual lift   off
of rare birds.

He waits.

Behind him,
spruce wood curls

into an idea

that leaps, catching on
airborne debris.

A form rises

as charred sparks
claw at air,

blackened sticks
splinter,

puffing up plumes

of red and gold.

The phoenix unfurls
the fan of its wings,

ascending from charcoal.

With his back turned,
the man searches

for birds he can't find

in the sky.

THE LYREBIRD

composes himself
on a mound of dirt.

He fans out his instrumental
tail,
soliciting attention
from potential mates

by reciting an arrangement.

Impersonating   perfectly
ordinary sounds—

chainsaws, car alarms,
the snick-snick of a whipper-snipper
            trimming underbrush,
a truck backing up—*beep*
                                        beep
                                                beep—
            a busy signal.

Trying to connect
with the chatter-crowded air,
he receives silence
from his species.

The lyrebird is out of tune.

He hangs on,
waiting for answers.

No one returns his calls.

AN UNORTHODOX GUIDE TO THE WILDLIFE OF NEW BRUNSWICK

Through Maine, there'll be moose, Canadian on this side.
Ignore the signs for the candy factory 40 miles on.
They're delusional. Also, the dragon at St. George.
Entering the city, there's a toll bridge, no trolls.
–Anne Compton (from "How to Get to Saint John")

Crows, sentinels along the border,
patrol the plunging telephone wires.
Whales slip under the invisible boundary line
not paying tariffs on meat they catch—
same with crabs and shellfish, scuttling
over international rocks after the flood tide.
Before crossing, fill up on cheap gas,
duty-free liquor and milk, though there's so many cows,
you can play connect-the-dots on their hides.
Through Maine, there'll be moose, Canadian on this side.

Legs like stampeding stilts on the highway,
they're better seen at the local zoo
(it borders the Rod & Gun Club).
Take an eggnog-fueled skate
at midnight on the lake—you'll dance
with deer snacking on crew-cut lawns.
In the barn, there's a horse with a horn

of light filtering through hay-strewn rafters.
You should see it: unicorns are rare, almost gone.
Ignore the signs for the candy factory 40 miles on.

Also, markers for the scenic drive—
it's all fog. Lots of apples, snakes won't mislead you,
except for the paramedic symbol on ambulances
hissing over ice-bitten roads; wheels
squeezing the life out of porcupines,
groundhogs. Next stop: by the gorge,
a house stockpiled with road kill.
Have some squirrel stew, then peek into
the residents' freezer. It's like a morgue of minced meat—
they're delusional. Also, the dragon at St. George,

though the menu at their Chinese restaurant
claims it's my horoscope. The French insist
that Vautours are vultures; the real birds here
are punk street pigeons, seagulls orbiting
flocks of steel cranes—halted on the harbour front,
red-white necks no longer fishing shoals
of asbestos. Underneath, union workers
and management head-butt like billy goats, gruffly,
trying to patch up this port town's rusty holes.
Entering the city, there's a toll bridge, no trolls.

TWO STREET PERFORMERS IN OAXACA

The pigeon lurches
along the ledge.

Chaplin-shuffling,
scoffing crumbs,
he continues his trampy act,
sidestepping
an Aztec statue
adorned in jaguar armour.

The sculpture holds
a notched sword
of obsidian triangles—

used when
gruesome monsoons
of knives and spears
flooded deserts.

The helmet's enormous
incisors grin.
The warrior kneels

—pulling his palm
from under
the speckled cloak.

He presents
an offering:

a heart, cut

from cardboard.

Bobbling back
across the stage,
the pigeon's eyes

sparkle in glee:
the vaudeville comic chuckles
at the seedy charade.

PENGUINS

Penguins parade around
dressed up as birds.

In a stiff-winged flurry,

they huddle together,
fighting the cold

fact:
they cannot fly.

The group
finds a gap
in the creaking ice,
and one by one,
skedaddle into the ocean.

No longer grounded

                    underwater,

the black-tie torpedoes
rocket around currents,
veering circles,
before
          plunging
                    up
                              and

out

into air.

Suspended

for a few seconds,

penguins skid on ice,
shaking off

the limits of
black and white.

THE FISHERMAN

The fisherman paces docks, by-passing boats
lit here and there by sputtering lamps.
Hunching his neck into his silver coat

furred with droplets from mist,
he notes others taking inventory: tugging
mesh nets, slinging coils. Twisting

ropes splash into the sea. The grey
fisherman stretches long legs,
steps into mirror water. Claws clutch clay,

pearl eyes scan the seabed.
Poised, lance angled down,
he lingers, stalking fish. Cocked head

calculates refraction. Strikes
with spear. Skewers feast.
The needle-nose sniper

flips its mackerel—lustrous scales swirl.
Throws its throat back. Swallows.
The glass surface fragments as the fisherman unfurls

wings, rowing forward in flight.
His cry ricochets off low clouds,
disappearing into the abyss of night.

THE THREE ORDERS OF GULLS IN ST. JOHN'S

I

The flock mobs the mall.

Wings beating
over scraps,

they hope to rise
in the pecking
order. Fast-food leftovers

(grease-soaked burgers,
          soggy fries)
are today's hot items,

and the gullible
          consumers
are ready to rip
                    apart
everything between them
and the best deal
          of the garbage.

II

At the dump,
seagulls
skim signs
posted by the higher-ups:

no loitering,
no scavenging,
offenders may be denied
future entrance.

They hover over it
for a moment,

then decide to settle on

the warning. Notice
the tarnished feathers,
reputations
plunging toward the land-
fill.

III

Over the sea,
          gulls spiral:
crosses stitching the sky
together. Almost holy.
          Rollers curl

under birds
          on gusts.

But they harbour
no thoughts.
It's beneath them.

RIFF ON A CHAMELEON

The chameleon unpacks
a kaleidoscope of colours,

summons some drowsy electric blues,
he moves—all static,

meditating on his new hues,

his constant devotion
to change.

MILITARY SURVIVAL TRAINING

A recruit is deserted in the woods, with bare
provisions: bowl, knife, matches, and a hare
his squadron hand-fed for a year. He cuts a stick
from a tree with the knife. The white
hare flattens its ears—hearing a hawk scream,
its nostrils quiver like a motor. It knows

the hawk is a predator. The recruit knows
the hare is defenceless; he can't bear
to abandon his pet to the screaming
bird's curved talons and beak. He holds the hare
under his arm, treading snow beneath white
trees. He scrapes at frozen moss with the stick.

He makes some moss tea, stirring with the stick.
For three days the recruit drinks tea. He knows,
as he huddles for warmth with the white,
furry hare—his aching stomach can't bear
more thin tea. He thinks of the fleshy hare,
thinks of eating his pet. He starts screaming

at the hare, driving it away with screams.
The recruit pokes the hare with the stick—
begging it, crying for the gentle hare
to try to run away from him, knowing
it will stay. He bludgeons the hare, can't bear
the kicking and struggling; bloodshot whites

of its eyes, brown irises, rolling; white
snow tarnished with red blood. The recruit screams—
the hare's ears droop. He skins the body bare
of fur, pulling pelt from muscle. Sticky
blood coats the knife. The recruit knows
the floundering fire won't stew the hare.

The water's hardly lukewarm. The hare
meat is tough, peppered with fur and white
bones. The recruit gorges, knowing
all that's left: moss that won't scream
when crushed for tea. He licks sticky
fingers clean of meat until the skin's bare.
The recruit, remembering the hare's screams,
buries the white bones, the knife, the stick,
leaving no witnesses to the death he bears.

BUT MY HORN SHALT THOU EXALT
(PSALM 92:10)

See the flicking tail that twirls.
See the trunk that pulls and curls.

See the wrinkles of many years.
See the flapping map-shaped ears.
See, a rumbling truck appears:

See the money, green and gold;
See the piano keys, yellow, old.
See the hand-carved ivory bowl.

See the rice and white chopsticks.
See the young girl's bright hair clips.
See dainty hands that lose their grip.
See, this is how the sculpture slips.

See it crash, break into chunks.
See his priceless piece of junk.

AQUARIUM

Inside this transparent circle of walls: Walls
monumental fractured columns, petrified   petrified
stalks of plants. We pass useful hours,   our
swirl in whispering circles for days,   days.

circulating past plastic skulls in coral tombs;   Tombs,
over rotten chests spewing money, jewels;   jewels,
phosphorescent volcano and castle.   castle—
We curl through this landscape in a haze   a haze.

of bubbles, gulping. Paper-thin sprinkles drift,   Drift,
twirling above us until they sink, settling   settling.
on the pink pebbled carpet. Humans mimic   Mimic
our sucked-in, eroded cheekbones; eyes gaze   gaze.

at us flickering by. Frothing water flows   Flow
from translucent tubes—in, out, comes, goes.   goes.

THIEF ON THE RANCH

The jaguar never
sees the longhorn cattle,

nor
the hot bang
that blossoms red
over black rosette pattern
dappling underbrush.

Mouth gaping into dark,
the cat limps on stained paws.

Falls
with a

whump

into dust.

The rancher stages the scene
for the photograph,

and in a flash, the shutter
captures his shadow

as the pelt unspools
into undeveloped silver.

GIRAFFE

The high-minded
mammal ascends
as a ruler

made of puzzle pieces.

His measured feet
overstep others

as he brushes twigs off
with his tongue
until he's full of it.

Coming down
from such a lofty

position is difficult:

he's willing to lower himself
only to risk a sip
from his likeness

in the water.
Drinking it up,

he loses his balance,

              falling

almost
into his own image.

The sun-spotted narcissist
is in peril,

he's so bent
on his own reflection.

NORTHERN GOSHAWK IN THE SALMONIER NATURE PARK

Watch out for the sniper.

Outfitted in uniform

grey, he's on guard atop
the wooden post.

See how, even still, the bird's

unstable. After this one run-in

with a power line, his wings

were set with pins,
but

he never recovered.

He's not

the straight shooter
he used to be.

Small things set him off.

A stick cracks.

The goshawk reacts

with cock-eyed aim,
taking a clumsy shot

at what he did before.

Launching an attack,

                    screeching,

fast,
against the fence. Links

ping. Again
and again,   ricocheting,

the raptor keeps grilling
himself, pushing his boundaries.

In his pent-up rage,
the truth
          escapes

him. Wiped out
          from fighting

a one-sided
skirmish,
          he retreats.

Returns

to his post.
Stands at attention.

The goshawk dismisses

his broken

wings, unflappable.

AN ACCIDENT

Steering blind,
the moose veers:

his turn
                                        onto the highway

gives no thought to body
          or logic.

The ruminant rising
from the ditch
is a clumsy spectacle—

he bursts   dancing
through a windshield

as the road forks
into antlers   now branching
the surface
of the sedan's backseat.

Sorting out the aftermath,
the animal is a pile-up
of leftover parts:

the baggy bell,
scissor-blade legs,
half a camel

hump—

when you put it together,
it's clear
the whole thing

is a mistake.

REASONS FOR FIRE IN THE ROCKIES

Flames
reconfigure mountains:
hypnotic ranges

of colour
transform topography.

Lively forms
flicker   across
vertical rock faces as dragons, obscured by flames,
scale switchbacks, and

only the opaque
gusts
assure me the flames haven't climbed
out
          of the
                    atmosphere
                                        altogether.

All routine and protocol,
the local guide offers
rationales for fire:

arson,
lightning,
prescribed burns—

the truth

vapourizes

in a whiff of fir smoke.

For him, the mystery of such space
is that nothing is hidden.

OLD WORLD SAND BOA

Raising only his head
from his burrow,

he waits for the sun
to find him.

Rustling
          diagonally
                                        over
                              the
          sand,

the reptile
          breeds messages—

not modern, in a way,
but similar to calligraphic scripture.

Its skin is printed with
cryptic patterns
          of jagged
                                        lines,
diamonds.

Inside his hypnotic eye:
a shivering shrew.

The velvet fork flicks

drifts of a dead
vocabulary.

A lick
insists:

a bite.

Blood snakes
in dark tongues

as exquisite points of incisors
          hook.

The muscular mosaic
curls,
          grips,
rendering the rodent
          into food.

Retreating into its den,
the boa's black markings

scribble an epitaph
in the dark.

FOR THE GREAT SHARK (NOT NECESSARILY WHITE)

For he is a bull, ramming bottoms of boats with his
heavy head.
For he can bang his head like a hammer.
For he tears through water like a torpedo.
For he is an expert at pool and hockey.
For he is a bizarre merry-go-round, insanely snapping
and whirling over land, when sucked into
a tornado.
For he is an ill-conceived tentacled menace when bred
with an octopus.
For he nearly drags the old man into the sea.
For he is a dreadful horror to Arthur Gordon Pym.
For he cruises along the sand, smooth silver-blue hide
rushing,
then pounding,
fin breaking like a blade on the
surface
in a hypnotic rush of
water.
For his eyes are carved from chipped obsidian glimmer.
For his teeth are mountains, rising from the depths; his
throat a dark gorge.
For he appears out of the dark, sharp head knifing,

cutting water when he locates a scent.

For his huge body lifts, flinging spray from fins, tail
lashing air.
For his jaws hook the fish with a clicking chop.
For he saws through meat with swept-back, serrated
teeth.
For he shakes his head again and again,
wrenching meat loose
from the fish
stuck
in swallowing jaws.
For he crashes down in a curtain of pink foam,
a mist plume staining the tide with
rising blood.
For he is ancient, the perfect predator at the top of
the food chain.
For his fins are precious jewels harvested for shark-
fin soup.
For he is skinned with a hot metal blade, then
dumped back into water, mutilated.

THE POINTER WIFE

The grey-haired woman growls
in the light of a gas lamp.
She pivots her pointer-head,
dented nose snuffling.

Eyes the colour of a fallen oak leaf
            detect her mate,
who hobbles on a thin stick
staunching a wound in his arm.

The hot copper blood
tarnishes the kitchen floor
that is chill in the shadows.

She growls at him.
What he used for gauze:
a handmade quilt
            she stitched herself.

She dampens a string through yellowed teeth
with stiff and dense fingers.

After all the times she sewed him up,
she's still jolted
seeing his skin
scarred and sutured

like squares of discordant cloth.

How many times,
she snarls,
did she ask him?

And why
can't he be more careful?
And how come
he can't give it up?

The needle
zigzagging
in the air like a dragonfly.

She nips the stray ends shut
and curtly repents for her clumsy claws.

Predatory in her humped stance,
she kneads elastic dough
with knotted knuckles:
yeasty bread that will soon unfurl
a soft, warm banner of revolt.

ROCKY HARBOUR BLUE WHALE

The dampened spirit
plunges under
                                        thunderclaps
of ice.

Water floods
bronchial trees,

submerging the mammal
for months,

until creaking floes
release
the whale:

a great breakthrough
on the pebbled beach.

The Atlantic salts the dark
forms:

people swarming in grey lines
snap cameras,

spout inflated concerns
around the foul carcass.

The entire situation is overblown.

The crowd cringes

as the flensing knife

punctures ventral pleats,
deflating the tension.

Dismantling the barnacle-spackled hull,
crews pack
all the nautical
nuts and bolts—

tail blades and fins,
joints, sockets,
propeller-shaped vertebrae—

into containers and onto trucks.

Then, in air-conditioned air,
cetologists assemble the skeleton.

Threaded on thin wire,
the vessel hangs
from the ceiling,

with the fragile,
unquestionable

transcendence
found in museums.

What remains

is, of course, rubbish.

In a loader bucket,
the real heart
of this wreck—

the aorta's tunnels—
rise
before

falling

at last
to rest

in the local dump.

HOW TO GET A CLAM TO OPEN UP TO YOU

Strewn over dunes, old bowls
hold hollowed-out promises
of food. They're hard cases—

the buried recluses
gush secrets. On top,
it's all hush-hush,

but from time to time, a tip-off
spurts out of mud.

A bit of digging unearths
the underground culture.

Snappy, the introverts
shut up. Thin-lipped smiles
disclose: they don't easily open
to others,

but a few figure
how to pry
into their lives.

A skilled locksmith, the heron
picks the slit
with flick-knife

precision until it unhinges.

A racoon draws his dagger
claws: after a few stabs
at the break-in, finally
sucks it up, stealing
away with the goods.

A young otter
finds the clam
a tough customer—

the unsolicited visitor
wallops the mollusc's shell.
          Shocked,

the clam's grin
is shattered
by the hard truth

as it hits rock
bottom.

THE BUTTERFLY

Backlit,
its body is an erratic

    shadow in flight, an aimless
intelligence picking up

    a pattern, deciding to be
    somewhere felt, but remote.

Please come back. You don't
want to go
out there, all crooked

with your numbered days.

WAYWARD GOOSE IN WINTER

I

Slow snow falls in a fog from branches,
sugar-coating the ice cakes that crash:
shards on the shore of the blue pond.

A goose struggles down the bankside,
webbed toes squirming in almost-frozen mud.
The arching black neck a question mark

punctuating the obvious: *What are you staring at?*
Whispers of its feeble flute drift
above cedar spires shrouded in snow.

Frosted needles shiver in the wind.
Spectral figures huddle over the goose,
who searches for a pale place in the sky.

II

Warm air and sun unlock the ice
around its hollow bones, releasing the goose
into the space where it failed to alight.

Red-winged birds pirouette in the dripping breeze:
cardinals, flickering fire on weeping branches,
candles lit in remembrance.

SEA URCHINS

cling to the brink
of isolated pools:
micro-communities
developing between salt-crusted
rocks. At low tide,
the spurs bristle
at peckish fowl,
and struggle
to turn back.
Shards
of ocean
recede:
moving on land
is a prickly issue,
and they get swept up
quick by plucky
birds,
until the last holdouts
are removed.

Whisked away
without ceremony,
the urchins are
swallowed—
their scattered
remains displaced inland,

over hills,
out of coves,
far from hissing surf.

A few still
litter the cliffs,

but there's little
to be salvaged,

just husks. Spiky arms
of dark stars—fallen
salutations of rejected points,

the inhabitants
cleaned out.

WASP NEST

The beach-combing armadillo's
earth-caked hand
cuffs the nest,
ripping apart the piñata shell.

He gobbles grubs
sprinkled with grey dust.

Almost weightless,
this foul globe
contains complex cells, subdivisions

of the maligned community.

Insects labour amid ramshackle
layers of papier-mâché:

mandibles scrape fibres,
mix wood, cardboard, saliva,
spit pulp.

Yellow-jacketed
architects hum,
tuning up the
colony's defense:
this fragile,

eerie, structure.
Keeping
in and out,

they repair
summer's tattered archaeology.

COCOON

Needles glint,

knitting. A nest
of silk fibres

cocoons
Nan from the world.
She can't remember anymore:

it's a scarf.
She's forgotten

the beginning

and keeps spinning
            the yarn,

threading tenuous
            connections.

Behind spectacles,
she squints, bug-eyed,
probing for something

recognizable to emerge:
a metamorphosis.

She's shaky, now

caught up
on a single
strand.

Fluttering,
    her fingers
    unable to grasp
what they once could,

she struggles
to pull a knot—loose
        ends of her memories   slip
    through the holes.

She clenches
    her knuckles

but the ball
    escapes,

    falls away.
        It rolls
        and rolls,

                        unravelling

everything

she

holds.

HAVANA

Angling, three men
tug and struggle against
the weight of pulleys hoisting ropes.
Poles bob, braced,

wait for a snap of

the deck, the lines,
stretched to their breaking
point. But they have a

hold: shaky, steady
now, guiding it into the air, reeling
they jig the fridge

onto the top-floor flat.
The catch here

is that there's no boats.
Except for the police
and the prohibited

rafts of trash:
tape strapped around
cola bottles, inner tubes, cast-off

plastics, drift, out for all

that's left: some kind of grouper, flat-faced

bottom feeders. The authorities
overlook the gathering of those   low-down scum
suckers, or even they'd have no fish at all.

THE PEACOCK AT THE ZOO

The blue-green bird with its waggling walk
mirrors the fronds of palm trees above,
or swirling sea algae stuck to stones in the marine exhibit.

A gold plaque declares:
peacocks reside in parties
where these poultry snap up frog's legs, insects—

cultivating the outrageous traditions
customary to the rich, including the harem of hens,
dull fluttering servants in the bejeweled bordello.

It also informs that wild birds occasionally
endure obligatory wrestles with jaguars,
staging a Pollock piece of abstract agony:

contorting circles of gold and black
whirling around a brilliant blue splash,
a frenzied merry-go-round of marks.

Scattered scratches from black talons and beak
clash with ragged rips of white teeth,
the whole composition spattered with red.

At last the feathered creature emerges
from the thick-trunked forest,
its triumphant train adorned by

blood-clotted turquoise fronds,
lumpy mascara on a thousand angry eyes,
like the headdress of an ancient Aztec after battle.

Here, the iridescent idol struts the concrete paths
of this caged kingdom without harm—or so I assumed,
until under a tungsten streetlight, I saw how some tires

burned a ribbon of rubber on the road,
the broken bird
a fractured Christmas ornament.

Smoke from the brakes floats straight up in the air,
so still the scene seems to hang like thread
from the mute darkness.

OCEAN

Orbiting birds drop like hammers
into pitching water.
Black rocks, plastered with seaweed,
are basins for tide pools.
Crowded by barnacles,
periwinkles, sea urchins—
ocean's spindled ragamuffins,
the stressed-out sea cucumber
squirts its insides out.

Clams buried in mud flats shoot jets of water—
a splash-pad for diggers.
On the pier, an otter curls like a slinky
into water where fish sparkle—
cascading jewels of sapphire, silver, gold.

From here, the ocean is a zoo:
elephant fish and horse fish;
hog- and frog- and dogfish;
even a unicorn fish.
The bigger fish have hatchets,
saws,
swords;
but the needle-nosed narwhal
could skewer all,
except maybe

the bony-jawed angler,
or fish made of translucent jelly,
rays that sting worse than wasps.

But every fish darts away from
those jagged cliffs of white teeth
lurking in the depths.

The bottom, dark as silt,
is lit only by luminous worms
(the thickness of a hair),
kaleidoscopic cuttlefish,
hissing electric eels.
An octopus curls tentacles
around bottles, boots,
a sunken coconut—
treasures from the ribcage of a rusted shipwreck
haunted by vampire squid,
ghostfish,
rainbow-hued coffin fish.

Bulbous blobfish
scowl like disgruntled clowns
at crustaceans. Here,
crabs are king or nomadic hermits
(occasionally, made of porcelain);
the punching mantis shrimp,
world champion boxer.

Rising whales pass squid—
Giant!

(*No, colossal!*)

The whales move
up,
up,
up,
then squirt parasols of water
into terrestrial wind,
gushing rumours of tentacular mythical beasts.

Seagulls settling on orange buoys echo the sun—
rise and sink, sink and rise.

ROCK AND GEM SHOP, BANFF

Fossils gathered
ages into the atmosphere

provide a fortune of
ancient geometries:
extinct cephalopods,
miniscule prehistoric fish,

a nautilus crafted
on the golden ratio.

Merchants rip off
these relics,
cheating the original
ancient stonecutters
                                        (gravity, pressure, time)
of millions of years' work.

Below mountains,
stores angle
bits of history
into kitsch.

Trilobites tilt on shelves,

their value sinking lower
than sea level.

THE TERRARIUM

attempts to cultivate
the desert's resilience.

Everything inside
is sharp, serrated:
a hostile ecosystem

maintained by heat
lamps mimicking the sun.
The threat of power failure

keeps the delicate arrangement
in permanent peril.
Still, not quite—

with a vicious backward jerk,
the lizard remains
resistant to meddling.

Leather chin flat,
he defends his artificial
territory with a thin smile.

DESERT

Off the tire-scarred road,
scarce signs

of humans:

an ax-split cross,
its arms strapped
with twine.

Shadows of telephone poles

string a thin line together,
reaching out beyond the horizon.
You think you can see past travellers. At sundown,
silhouettes shape illusions

of pitching homesteads, ranches
with cowboys and Mexican
horse thieves.

Spokes wheel wagons
with oxen, herds
of cattle. Abandoned

carcasses time-lapse
into peroxide skeletons.

That's a dead end romanticized.

Turn back. Only the severe resist

the friction of dirt whips
lashing iron-rich rocks.
At the edge of foothills:

the saguaro's
two arms

brace against the bloody
red rising moon:

a newfound evangelical being
conveyed
down
the mountain
to save
the survivors
of the desert. Scrub
bristles
as snakes unravel
stale skins—rags inhabited

only in passing.
Woodpeckers and owls
defy the point

of cacti: well-armoured

nests offer perches
to plunge at skittish

reptiles. Shrugging off old tails,

lizards scrabble
up the makeshift pulpit,

pursuing arachnids.
Spiders, scorpions flee
exoskeletons,

for their dot-to dot
holes punched into the earth.

Everything regenerates,
believing new beginnings

will save them.

ACKNOWLEDGMENTS

Earlier versions of some of these poems appeared in *Pulp Literature* and *Newfoundland Quarterly*.

Special thanks to Mary Dalton, who has supported and accepted me and my work for several years. I thank her for her encouragement, inspiration, advice, and love of cats and all creatures in general. To Mr. Browne, for his fascinating stories of old St. John's, which inspired several pieces of non-fiction. Also to Sharon McCartney for helping with words and ideas, and opening up her house in Fredericton to me. And to my husband, Mike, for assisting with many late-night edits, putting up with papers and art littering the house, and living with far too many pets.

KATIE VAUTOUR

Katie Vautour is a visual artist and writer published in a variety of literary journals, and though she dabbles in all genres (including fiction, non-fiction, and playwriting), her main focus is poetry. She is also the director of the Piper's Frith Writing Retreat. Katie graduated from the Nova Scotia College of Art and Design University with majors in Filmmaking, Painting, Drawing, and Art History. She has participated in residencies in Oaxaca, Mexico; New Brunswick; and the Banff Centre. She exhibits her mixed-media work, paintings, and drawings throughout Atlantic Canada, and gladly repurposes used materials into art. She lives in St. John's.